Projecting Phoebe

Maria Iskander

BookLeaf Publishing
India | USA | UK

Presentation by *BookLeaf Publishing*

Web: www.bookleafpub.com

E-mail: info@bookleafpub.com

ISBN: 9789357446693

First edition 2022

DEDICATION

I dedicate this book to my selfless, ingenious and generous father- Dr Philip Iskander.

ACKNOWLEDGE MENT

Maria Iskander acknowledges the Aboriginal and Torres Strait Islander Elders past, present and future. From the stories, traditions and living cultures of Aboriginal and Torres Strait Islander peoples on this land, I am committed to play my part in building a brighter and sustainable future together.

Stronger

Every day's been inching to.
These final exams that I must do.
The stress is there but I choose to have peace.
You are with me and will never leave.
I'm not asking You to make it easier.
But I plead You to make me stronger.

Shine Your light on me and my mind.
Help me, guide me to do one of a kind.
I'm not asking You to make it easier.
But I plead You to make me stronger.

This season of study is coming to an end.
I am slightly afraid , I can't pretend.
Please bless me with Your grace.
Make me brave in every place.
I'm not asking You to make it easier.
But I plead You to make me stronger.

I want to do well for Your glory, not mine.
Please make me capable of doing fine.
There is no substitute nor someone else,
You are all I've got, You have always been my help.
If it wasn't for You, I would come to rejection.

You give my life purpose and direction.
So right now I'm anticipating these finals soon.
May I keep trusting in Your promises and love for me too.
For I know You can't make it easier.
But You will be with me and make me stronger

We are all Human

Where do we catch our breath?
Where can we draw the line?
Another terror has taken place.
Once again taking innocent lives.

It may not be Christians,
Still the death stings pure.
Muslims and Christians in Egypt.
Both humans are the same with a different core.

Indeed we are different in religion.
Yet we as humans, bleed just the same.
We are loved by God our Creator.
Who for we the sinners, freely forgave.

His Son Jesus, tasted our humanity and shared our pain.
He experienced grave loss and how human loss can maim,
Yet, in His love for all of us, He gives us a solution.

Our lives need only to taste a temporary void or confusion.
As the solution is to will and take peace from God, not devilish fear.
God's not dead and He's not deaf to any of our cries or tears.
It pains Him more than one can credits God or imagine to be,
When HE sees His creation suffer from vile attacks of inhumanity.

We are all fallen and broken in some way or another.
Although it's never easy, may we still keep by each other.
No difference in skin, or religion or belief can ever justify.
The spiteful killings of humans in this present day and time.
Everyone's life is precious and well deserving to live.
Dear God, the Father of us all, teach us how to be brave and forgive.

Own it

When the sadness comes, acknowledge it.
Greet it and prepare for it to leave soon.
Once owning it, let it go and be free.

God made you for a purpose.
God's grace exceeds the surface.
You are precious and beloved.
Never lose faith or ever stop it.

People may rejoice at your misery.
Those people will receive one epiphany.
For God is not unjust to accept their evil.
God will help you show them and stand tall.

Try not to be concerned, for the world has come to,
More people wishing bad than good, towards me and you.
So my dear, own the good and bad just the same.
As God's hand in your life will bring glory- not shame.

To get to You

Such a sublime blessing you have gifted.
A perfect peace, with no limits.
You'd walk to the end to find me.
You forgive me , even when I'm angry.
The means to get to You , is all I ever want.

There are days I feel over it
Struggling to cheerfully submit.
My stubbornness is deceivingly sweet.
But I know in the end, it profits nothing.

The days go more than I keep up.
I want to grow but sometimes I'm stuck,
Stuck in a plateau of religious rules,
Forgetting what it means to really love You.

One's got to change very much.
Each day is a chance for a new start.
I know in the end it will be worth it all.
The means to get to You , is all I ever want.

Anzac Day Poem-
100 Years Milestone

This 25th of April marks 100 years of the iconic annual ANZAC day- a day of great remembrance;
For all the strong and courageous soldiers, both Australian and New Zealander,
This is no day of mere celebration, but of national memory;
We must learn and learn again, from the mistakes of this infamous war,
That we are one in the spirit and one in the Lord.

This is a day to know, and to appreciate, how precious this blessed country Australia truly is.
So without further ado let us all now pray with Reverence.
For God to bless and reward the ANZACs immensely for what they've done.
The soldiers 'great sacrifice, has and will forever impact their families, Australia, and everyone.
The ANZACS walked by and by one another,

Standing strong side by side, and worked with each other
Guarding each other's dignity and always saving each other's pride,
All of these selfless sacrifices and great humilities
Are living proof that we should take by their example in walking one in spirit and in the Lord.

These legendary soldiers will never ever be forgotten,
After all, how can we ever forget those who died for us?
You ANZACs were the beautiful people in this harsh world and life,
And you can only be felt in our hearts, not merely just seen or heard alone.
For you fought the good fight and never gave in til the final breath.
You have walked in true spirits and in the name of the Lord.

Addiction

Tablets scattered on the table and the floor,
I think we've become addicted to some kind of temporary fix or relief from pain
We find ourselves sooner before we know it, trapped in a destructive path like this.
Addicted to the lies this is for their benefit, it is simply innocent.
These lies that keep feeding our souls and keep us deceived that this blanket for pain is fine,
After all, what harm can this tiny capsule do, but give a little comfort from some misery,
But truth be told, it is actually killing us slowly and steadily.
No one will ever know and no one needs to, we say,
I think we are scared of admitting that we lost our way.
People be quick to judge your actions regardless of it being good or bad,
This shouldn't phase us too much, we must learn to care far more to pleasing not people – but more our Heavenly Dad.

It is not the end if we fall in this or any kind of mistake,
After all the true tragedy is not falling into sin, the real tragedy is not getting out of it.
God waits for us every day to turn back to Him and accept His grace and forgiveness, for our failures.
All we need to do is to tell Him by both words and actions, that we accept our freedom through Him.
A freedom that is not based on doing whatever we want and living entirely as we choose,
But a kind of freedom to live in the God-inspired way- that is to strive, to live the way we ought to.

I love you,Egypt!

I Love my Egypt
Egypt the country of the golden sand,
The Country that follows God's command;
The place where people oughta want to see,
And admire its beauty, from the land, to the Red sea.

On the 6th of October the Great day or Remembrance;
For all the Egypt soldiers, we prayed with Reverence.
For God to always protect them for what they've done.
For their families, for Egypt, and for everyone.

Egypt, Oh Egypt, how we all Love Egypt;
Jesus, Our Lord used to walk around its very lands.
It's the place where it fully relies on God's special plan.
For it to always be able to safely get through.

Oh Egypt, Our Country Egypt, How we all Love You.

In 2011 the official Revolution began.
With protests and melodies that the people sang;
That attacked the government and all its terrible ways.
That time was the birth, for people, finally having a say.

The Uprising won, but had its flaws.
'Cause when Mubarak was gone, Morsi took the floor.
He ruled over Egypt like a puppet with a string.
He cared for nothing for Egypt, or anything.

Egypt, Oh Egypt, how we all Love Egypt;
Jesus, Our Lord used to walk around its very lands.
It's the place where it fully relies on God's special plan.
For it to always be able to safely get through.
Oh Egypt, Our Country Egypt, How we all Love You.

The year 2013 was the year with continuous strife.
Till the great day, when we finally won the fight.
Morsi had to also leave presidency and resign,

So finally now a respected leader could be assigned.

Egypt deserves the very best.
No more fighting or religious prejudice, but rest.
And peace, hope and faith that it deserves more.
With a great president who'll help it soar.

Egypt, Oh Egypt, how we all Love Egypt;
Jesus, Our Lord used to walk around its very lands.
It's the place where it fully relies on God's special plan.
For it to always be able to safely get through.
Oh Egypt, Our Country Egypt, How we all Love You.

People Will

‘People will fail you. There is no doubt about it.

People will hurt you. Just go with that.

People will burn you, until there's nothing left.

People will try to disturb you, with words
unmet.

For the people that are evil like days on end.
For the people who destroy you, like a slaughter
to a lamb.
You all are needed for the law and order in this
world.
You all should know your place in the
afterworld.

Where will these terrible people go?
Where do these terrible people show?
Where are you?
Oh sorry , I didn't get that.
I guess your place in the afterworld,
Will come back to bite you- making you all sad.

No longer

I no longer want to keep playing to your evil schemes. I no longer want to partake in your fickle dreams. You always sugar coated the bad, making me a fool to believe you. So, I no longer will allow you, to use me as a tool. Get with it. We are done. I no longer want to see you. Or in fact, anyone.

She cried

Life getting her overboard.
She feels like a piece of dust, without a cause.
More people are mistaking her for a fool.
With their games and silly tools.
That made her feel ,
How she was no longer made of steel,
And so she cried.

Next day it only gets far worse,
Feels as if her plans are rehearsed,
You got the normal morning run,
And the simple things deemed 'fun'.
More broken did she feel,
For she was no longer made of steel,
And so she cried.

You see my fellow friends,
People say they knew you only when ,
You may later pass due to the hurt,
Or when they realise they treated you like dirt,
To be stepped on like it's normal to.
No one changes until it's' over due,
And they realise that they have lost you.
This world and its people have broken me,
I hope they now have the ability to feel

And to have realised , that I'm not made of steel,
Can you hear and see me now?
My time is up, so 'chow' my fellow friends, for now.
And this time , they cried.

You don't mean it

You say you want be friends and miss me dearly
Then I get your snaps of you at a party and it points to me clearly ,
That your words are empty and you’re playing games.
I need honesty and so don’t think that it’s me being anti-social or lame.
If I decline to come to your places, know that I can’t bother anymore,
With you, or your lies, that causes pointless problems- making my heart sore.

My eyes are finally open- for once I was blind.
So, now I know that you never meant what you said.
Your whole life was a "Hollywood soap scaled" lie.

You say I’m complicated,
Because I follow and understand your schemes,
You try and make me the problem
But no one is as dumb as you think,
Though the lies last for a bit,

The truth will always be revealed.
It shouldn't surprise you ,
When you find yourself unravelling from your seams.

My eyes are finally open- for once I was blind.
So, now I know that you never meant what you said.
Your whole life was a "Hollywood soap scaled" lie.

I need Your Love

Walking around in circles, losing sight of what I am supposed to do.
Running far and far away from You.
I am in need of some love.

I am fearful and feeling so confused more and more.
You say that you love me and always will forevermore.
But how do you love me, a broken soul?

Cry out to You

I cry out to you and it seems you don't care to hear me.
You have left me alone and pushed me too far.
On the ground, you watch me fall further into the deep.
I am losing sight of what your plan is for us and for me.
You say that to be with you, we must go through the narrow gate,
But I feel that You have abandoned me and my heart is about to break.
And as I continue to cry out again , to you, for just a simple answer or sign
You remain to stay far from me and give me no comfort of any kind.

The Problem

I finally received an epiphany today- hooray for
it!
I realized the problem was not what I expected.
The problem was not you being out of reach
from me.
The problem was me blocking You from my
heart.
And making you my enmity.

True Friends

Imagine what's more than getting all you want?
And imagine whose worth to open all your heart.
There are many times,
We don't ever understand.
Things that randomly happen
Changing our plans quickly.
Who can stay through it?
With you strong for so long.
Who'd never leave you alone?

Only true friends.
Stay in the good and bad.
They rejoice with you,
And grieve if you're sad.
Grateful for your worth.
As you are for theirs.
They challenge you to be your best.
Only true friends can love or understand,
Immeasurably like the grains of sand.

Indeed true friends are one of a kind.
And so, so very hard to find.
There is no price, silver or gold.
That'd replace my void of a good soul.
There is no treasure lying in this atmosphere.
Nothing's better than a true friend here.

She

She speaks loud and clear.
She smiles with no ounce of fear.
She is always there- even not physically.
Like a glue, she holds this family tight.
She's a very successful mum.
Overcomer of struggles - under the sun.

Achieving the impossible.
She has kept us safe, holy and humble.
A light to keep us from going blind.
She is a graceful flower- one of a kind.
Comforter for our silent sadness,
A rock in the loud madness.

She cares for us- way way overtime.
Her love for us goes the extra mile.
She is a good mother- trustworthy and kind.
She is a beacon of hope in the worst of times.

She is a cheerleader in our times of stress.
She always gives feelings of peace and rest.
She is a mother, like you and me.
She is a mother here for you- eternally.

Christmas Blessing for 2021

The Christmas Season comes but once a year.
A time to fill you and I, with love and cheer.
May this Christmas Season warm your home.
A time that glitters your path with hope.

Let this Christmas Season be a tender time to contemplate.
A time to be courageous to start a new slate.
Indeed, this Christmas Season, accounts our thanks to Christ.
A gentle reminder of His immaculate birth at night.

Christmas Season signifies our bigger intentions,
A time to draw near to God, and His divine interventions.
Therefore, our two wonderful gifts for you in 2021,
Is a love unfailing, and a peace that accepts each and everyone.

Pas' d' air (No Air)

I lay down and feel unrest.
Heart out and put to the test.
Stuck in here, deep down inside.
I am trying to stay positive all the time.
Can't complain, but I still bleed.
Missing your presence with me.

I miss Your aroma on my clothes.
I miss You seeing my weird toes.
I miss Your taste in my mouth.
I miss You from the inside out.

Shame is on me for not visiting enough.
Shame on me for not taking Your love.
I was not ready- never was.
So I would always delay.
The fear inside me, took a hold,
And so I kept running away.

Now, I'd do anything to see You,
To be cosy at Your place again.
I'd do anything to talk to You,
To have Your touch again.

The cruel irony of this very day, is this

A world brought to its knees, to a virus.
As people die from this virus, due to a lack of air,
Your absence from me is totally not fair.

My longing for you - even after You're gone,
Proves that I have been a fool all along.
I am a fool, I am a fool, I am a fool,
For thinking I could live without You.

Right Now

Right now , at this very moment, as you read these very words, know that God is still working and planning amazing adventures and chapters for your life. Right now, all you need to do is to play your part in your destiny. Right now, all you will do, is to strive for his symphony. For without striving, there is no trust, and without trust, there is no love. So what are you waiting for? The time for your heart's desires to be fulfilled, is RIGHT NOW.

What do you Value?

People value being true to themselves.
And some value impressing others.
People value doing good for social fame.
And some value doing good for humanity's sake.
People value being kind to others, and true.
And some value never spending money on you.
People value conforming to the lies.
And some value living in the truth- all of the time.

Seek first

Seek first to understand and employ empathy for
what strangers go through.
Seek first to respect and intrinsically appreciate
what others do for you.
Seek first to change and be accountable for
every action.
Seek first to be the start of a 'love' chain
reaction.
Seek first to love yourself when you feel
unlovable.
Seek first to nourish your faith, even when it's'
uncomfortable.
Seek first to intrigue others to grow in joy and
grace.
Seek first to leave your light, in every single
place.

www.ingramcontent.com/pod-product-compliance
Lightning Source LLC
Chambersburg PA
CBHW051748130826
49812CB00033B/1059
* 9 7 8 9 3 5 7 4 4 6 6 9 3 *